A Gifted Child in Foster Care:
A Story of Resilience

TEACHER'S GUIDE
REVISED EDITION

READING COMPREHENSION & CHARACTER EDUCATION
for Students

Written by
Dr. Grace LaJoy Henderson

THE LESSONS IN THIS WORKBOOK UST BE USED IN CONJUNCTICN WITH THE NONFICTION BOOK ENTITLED, A GIFTED CHILD IN FOSTER CARE: A STORY OF RESILIENCE - REVISED EDITION BY DR. GRACE LAJOY HENDERSON

***Inspirations* by Grace LaJoy**
Post Office Box 181
Raymore, Missouri 64083

This workbook must be used in conjunction with the nonfiction book, **A Gifted Child in Foster Care:** *A Story of Resilience* – REVISED EDITION

A GIFTED CHILD IN FOSTER CARE – TEACHER'S GUIDE – REVISED EDITION
Copyright ©2010, 2020. Grace LaJoy Henderson
Published by Inspirations by Grace LaJoy
Raymore, Missouri

ISBN 978-1-7341868-2-6

All rights reserved. No portion of this book may be copied, reproduced or transmitted in any form without prior written permission from the publisher.

Printed in the United States of America

TABLE OF CONTENTS

Testimonials	vi
A Word from the Author	vii
Introduction	viii
Reading Comprehension Skills	ix
To the Teacher – Character Trait, Theme, Mood, Problem, and Solution of story	x

Lesson One ………………………………………………………………………….. 1

- Main Idea and Supporting Details
- Sequencing
- Identifying Cause and Effect
- Interpreting and Evaluating Information
- Comparing and Contrasting
- Character Trait Discussion – *Appreciation*

Lesson Two …………………………………………………………………………… 5

- Main Idea and Supporting Details
- Sequencing
- Identifying Cause and Effect
- Interpreting and Evaluating Information
- Comparing and Contrasting
- Character Trait Discussion - *Honesty*

Lesson Three ………………………………………………………………………… 9

- Main Idea and Supporting Details
- Sequencing
- Identifying Cause and Effect
- Interpreting and Evaluating Information
- Character Trait Discussion - *Respect*

Lesson Four …………………………………………………………………………… 11

- Main Idea and Supporting Details
- Sequencing
- Identifying Cause and Effect
- Interpreting and Evaluating Information
- Comparing and Contrasting
- Character Trait Discussion – *Dependable*

Lesson Five 15

- Main Idea and Supporting Details
- Sequencing
- Identifying Cause and Effect
- Interpreting and Evaluating Information
- Comparing and Contrasting
- Character Trait Discussion - *Secure*
- Bonus Discussion

Lesson Six 19

- Main Idea and Supporting Details
- Sequencing
- Identifying Cause and Effect
- Interpreting and Evaluating Information
- Comparing and Contrasting
- Character Trait Discussion - *Love*

Lesson Seven 23

- Main Idea and Supporting Details
- Sequencing
- Identifying Cause and Effect
- Interpreting and Evaluating Information
- Comparing and Contrasting
- Character Trait Discussion - *Obedience*

Lesson Eight 27

- Main Idea and Supporting Details
- Identifying Cause and Effect
- Interpreting and Evaluating Information
- Comparing and Contrasting
- Character Trait Discussion - *Content*

Lesson Nine 31

- Main Idea and Supporting Details
- Sequencing
- Identifying Cause and Effect
- Comparing and Contrasting
- Character Trait Discussion - *Courage*

Lesson Ten **35**

- Main Idea and Supporting Details
- Sequencing
- Identifying Cause and Effect
- Interpreting and Evaluating Information
- Comparing and Contrasting
- Character Trait Discussion - *Encouragement*

Lesson Eleven **39**

- Main Idea and Supporting Details
- Sequencing
- Identifying Cause and Effect
- Interpreting and Evaluating Information
- Comparing and Contrasting
- Character Trait Discussion - *Diligence*

Lesson Twelve **43**

- Main Idea and Supporting Details
- Sequencing
- Identifying Cause and Effect
- Interpreting and Evaluating Information
- Comparing and Contrasting
- Character Trait Discussion - *Insight*

Lesson Thirteen **47**

- Interpreting and Evaluating Information
- Character Trait Discussion - *Forgiveness*

Lesson Fourteen **49**

- Interpreting and Evaluating Information
- Character Trait Discussion - *Building Self Esteem*

Bonus Character Trait Discussion – *Determination* **51**

Advanced Reading Comprehension Skills **52**

Additional Lesson Ideas **53**

Additional activity ideas that coincide with "A Gifted Child in Foster Care: A Story of Resilience", which may be used in conjunction with the Four Core Curriculum Areas: Language Arts, Mathematics, Science/Technology, and Social Studies; also Career Preparatory and Communication Arts/Journalism.

Testimonials

"It's a new way to implement nonfiction, character education and key reading strategies."
~**Suzanne Wiley**, Reading Specialist - Lee's Summit R7 School District

"If taken to heart, the Character Trait Discussions in this workbook, will result in a more resilient child who can overcome adversity." ~**Dr. Steve McClure**, Assistant Director - University of Missouri, Kansas City - Charter School Center

"The lessons in this workbook help students understand the reading better. The discussion questions help students apply the character traits to their own life." ~**Shardae Williams**, 7th Grade Student - Smith Hale Middle School

"Several reading comprehension skills are reinforced in every lesson, which helps students learn. The character trait discussions help students apply life skills and make connections to the text."
~**Jennifer Gooding**, Reading Intervention Teacher - Belton School District

"…an excellent tool for students to learn. The reading comprehension skills coincide with the Department of Education's curriculum expectations." ~**Celest West**, Reading Teacher – Center Alternative School, Kansas City, MO

A Word from the Author

When I was two years old, my mother left me and my five brothers and sisters and she never came back! She left us with our father. As a single parent, Daddy did his best to raise us and tried very hard to keep us together. But when I was seven years old, he ended up leaving me and four of my brothers and sisters in a house alone. He took my oldest brother, who was fifteen years old at that time, with him. The oldest child left in the house was my fourteen-year-old brother.

Daddy had promised to send money and he even asked his girlfriend Rose and my Aunt Mattie to check on us. But somehow, the house we were left in ended up with no lights, no gas, no phone, no water, and no food. Even the lock on the front door was broken, leaving me feeling afraid.

One late night, at about two o'clock a.m., the sheriff came and removed us all from that house. "We are taking you to an emergency foster home for a nice hot breakfast, "the sheriff said to me. Since I had not had a good meal for several weeks, I was happy to go.

I lived in foster care for three years. I experienced numerous ups and downs while living in foster care, but one of the things that sticks with me is the fact that my school placed me, a foster child, in the Gifted and Talented class. I did not understand why I was chosen because I did not feel smart at all. I felt like my gifted classmates deserved to be in that class, but I did not.

Daddy finally met the state's requirement to take us home to live with him when I was ten years old. We were stable for about six months, then he began taking us with him as he traveled from state to state. He finally stopped taking us with him when I was twelve, and I began living with my eighteen-year-old sister.

I lived with my sister until I was eighteen years old, at which time I became a single parent and began living on my own. It was hard being a single parent. I worked and went to school while raising my two children. Today, my two children have grown up to be responsible adults. Both of them graduated from high school and went to college.

I have earned my Doctorate degree and I am the author of over thirty books including book, **A Gifted Child in Foster Care:** *A Story of Resilience*. In this book, I expound on my story of being abandoned by my mother and father. I share intimate details about my life experience before, during and after foster care. I also offer words of empowerment to children and parents. This book has already gained the attention of foster care and adoptive organizations as well as educators worldwide.

Sometimes I wonder what my life would have been like with a mother. But, if my life story would have been different, I would not be the person I am today, and I like who I am today!

Dr. Grace LaJoy, Author
A Gifted Child in Foster Care:
A Story of Resilience

Introduction

This workbook includes important learning activities for every chapter of the *nonfiction* book "A Gifted Child in Foster Care: A Story of Resilience".

Students will learn these Reading Comprehensive skills:

- Identifying the Main Idea and Supporting Details
- Sequencing Events
- Identifying Cause and Effect
- Comparing and Contrasting
- Interpreting and Evaluating Information
- Identifying and Discussing Character Traits

Reading Comprehension Skills

Identifying the Main Idea and Supporting Details

The main idea is the most important part of the chapter. It is the main thought that the author is trying to get across to the reader. The rest of the chapter may contain details that support the main idea. The main idea may be found in any part of the chapter. More than one main idea may be found within a chapter.

Sequencing Events

Sequencing means to place information in a particular order. For example: Identifying what happened first, second, and third in the chapter.

Identifying Cause and Effect

Effect answers the question "What happened?" Cause answers the question "What made it happen?" or "Why did it happen?" Cause and effect may also include "Drawing Conclusions" or looking at something that has already happened and trying to figure out what is going to happen next.

Comparing and Contrasting

Comparing and contrasting means to identify what is the same and different about a person, place or thing. For example, two cars can be the same in some ways and different in others.

Interpreting and Evaluating Information

Interpreting and evaluating information includes reading a chapter and thinking carefully about what has been read. It also includes determining what is meant by the information in the chapter. A reader may examine information from a chart or a graph, then explain what it means.

Identifying and Discussing Character Traits

Identifying and discussing character traits include discovering virtues and attitudes of characters in the chapters. A Character Trait may be "respect". Identifying this trait may include discussing how "respect" is portrayed in a chapter. Readers may discuss how they may display "respect" towards themselves and others. The character trait discussion topics are designed to encourage students to advance to a higher level of critical thinking.

To the Teacher

A powerful memoir such as "A Gifted Child in Foster Care: A Story of Resilience" should do three things for students: Promote group discussion; Cause them to know that they can achieve success; Inspire them to write their own memoir.

Although the reading comprehension skills in this workbook are vital for increasing academic achievement, students also need the opportunity to make their own personal connections to the text. Here is how to help your students get the most out of this empowering story: First, allow students to read through "A Gifted Child in Foster Care: A Story of Resilience" for enjoyment; Second, encourage them to share, in a group setting, the personal connections they made to the story; Third, discuss the story's overall Character Trait, Theme, Mood, Problem, Solution and Main Characters (see below); Finally, lead them in practicing the reading comprehension skills that are comprised in this workbook.

The definitions and story details below will help you discuss the overall story with your students.

Character Trait describes behaviors, thoughts or feelings of the people in the story. It is one word such as "respect", "appreciation", or "love".

> The *Character Trait* for A Gifted Child in Foster Care is "Resilience". Resilience means to "bounce back" after a negative life experience. To live a successful life in spite of hardships.

Theme is the meaning, concept or message of the story. There may be more than one.

> The *Theme* for A Gifted Child in Foster Care is "Overcoming Adversity"/"Never giving up"

Mood is the feeling created in the reader. It also represents the feeling readers may uncover while reading the story. (for example: sad, happy, devastation, peaceful)

> The *Moods* for A Gifted Child in Foster Care are "Fear", "Insecurity", and "Forgiveness"

Problem is the issues or situations that are found in the story?

> The *Problem* in A Gifted Child in Foster Care is: The author was abandoned and experienced a turbulent life.

Solution is what happened, did not happen, or should have happened as a result of the problem?

> The *Solution* in A Gifted Child in Foster Care is: The author's needs were met in foster care; She later realized she had a gift to write and became a successful author.

Main Characters of the story:
Grace, Mother, Father, Grandmother, Big Mama

Lesson One

This lesson coincides with Chapter One of the book, A Gifted Child in Foster Care: A Story of Resilience
Chapter One – "Left by Mother"

Character Trait – "Appreciation"

Main Idea and Supporting Details

Place an "X" on the line beside the "main idea" of the story.

__X__ Mother left when Grace was two years old and never came back. (p. 7)

_____ Grandmother believed Grace was a strong and resilient child.

_____ Grace stayed home with her mother while her father worked.

The <u>four</u> statements below "support" the main idea. Fill in the blanks with the correct word.

The words "your mother doesn't want you" ___devastated___ Grace. (p. 7)

Grace was __embarrassed__ for her friends at school to know about her mother leaving. (p.8)

Grace remembers both __good__ and __bad__ things her mother. (p. 8)

Grace has gained a greater __appreciation__ for life because of her mother. (p. 13)

Sequencing

Place a "1" on the line beside the event that happened first in Chapter One.
Place a "2" on the line beside the event that happened second in Chapter One.
and so on...

__5__ Grace often wonders what type of life her mother is living (p. 13)

__3__ Grace's school mates asked, "Where is your mother?" (p. 8)

__6__ Grace feels a strong sense of love and loyalty towards her mother (p. 13)

__1__ Grace was born (p. 7)

__2__ Grace's mother left (p. 7)

__4__ Grace remembers a lot of things about her mother (p. 8)

A Guide to Reading and Comprehension & Character Education *for Students*
© Inspirations by Grace LaJoy

Identifying Cause and Effect

"Mother went out into the backyard one evening and lay down to hide in the tall, uncut grass because she feared being picked up by the state to be locked up again in a mental institution."

What is the cause?   Mother feared being picked up by the state to be locked up   (p. 13)

What is the effect?   Mother went out into the backyard and hid in the tall, uncut grass (p. 12)

Interpreting and Evaluating Information

Circle <u>all</u> of the feelings Grace experienced after her mother left. (p. 8) (p. 12 - devastation)

Devastation   Joy   **Embarrassment**   **Fear**   Guilt   **Insecurity**   Excitement   **Rejection**

Comparing and Contrasting

Name three(3) things that are different about these two stories from Chapter One

Mother made cookies (p. 9)	*Mother popped popcorn* (p. 10)
Grace sat on the porch	Grace took a bath
Grace never got cookies	Grace got popcorn
Siblings and neighbors ate the cookies	Neighbor boy took Grace's popcorn

Character Trait Discussion

The Character Trait for Lesson One is "Appreciation".

Appreciation means to feel "thankful".

Read the statement below. Then chose <u>one</u> of the questions below and answer it. Write your answer in the space provided then discuss it with your group.

Grace still loves and appreciates her mother even though she left her with her father and never came back.

1. Would you appreciate your mother if she left you and never came back? Why or why not?
2. Name a person who you appreciate. Why do you appreciate that person?
3. Why is it important to "appreciate" other people?

Answers will vary. No right or wrong answer.

Lesson Two

This lesson coincides with Chapter Two of the book, A Gifted Child in Foster Care: A Story of Resilience
Chapter Two – "Living with Daddy"

Character Trait – "Honesty"

Main Idea and Supporting Details

Place an "X" on the line beside the "main idea" of the story.

_____ Daddy enjoyed the blues, love songs and gospel music.

__X__ After Mother left, Daddy did all he could to care for his children. (p. 15)

_____ Daddy received help from Grace's Grandmother.

Write four "supporting details" for the main idea.

1. Daddy had a job pouring concrete sidewalks, steps, and driveways.   (p. 15)

2. On Fridays, Daddy bought home bags of food for the family.   (p. 16)

3. Daddy gave the children allowances.   (p. 16)

4. Daddy was patient.   (p. 17)

Sequencing

What did Daddy do after mother disappeared never to return? (p. 15)

Daddy faithfully committed his life to raising the children as a single parent.

Daddy did all he could to care for the children and keep them together.

Identifying Cause and Effect

Grace believed her mother left because Daddy abused her. (p. 15)

What is the "Cause"? Daddy abused Mother

What is the "Effect"? Mother left

Interpreting and Evaluating Information

What example did Grace write about, in Chapter Two, to show how determined she could be about a goal? (p. 17)

__She hid her cake in her shoe and told her father she ate it so she could sneak it outside to__

__eat it.__

Comparing and Contrasting

How was Daddy's treatment of Mother <u>different</u> from the way he treated the children. (p. 15)

__He abused mother, but he never struck the children.__

Character Trait Discussion

The Character Trait for Lesson Two is "Honesty"

Honesty means being truthful. Speaking the truth. Saying what is true.

Answer the <u>three</u> questions below. Write your answer in the spaces provided then discuss them with your group.

1. What was Grace's response when Daddy asked "Did you finish eating your cake?" __yes__ (p. 17)
2. Was her response "honest"? Why or why not?
3. Describe a time when you were honest <u>or</u> *not* honest. What happened as a result?

   __Answers will vary. No right or wrong answer.__

A Gifted Child in Foster Care – Teacher's Guide
© Inspirations by Grace LaJoy, LLC

Lesson Three

This lesson coincides with Chapter Three of the book, A Gifted Child in Foster Care: A Story of Resilience
Chapter Three – "Grandmother"

Character Trait – "Respect"

Main Idea and Supporting Details

Place an "X" on the line beside the "main idea" of the story.

_____ Daddy struggled to raise six children alone.

_____ Grace's first day of kindergarten was scary.

__X__ Grandmother played an important role in Grace's life. (p. 24)

Write three "supporting details" for the main idea.

1. __Grandmother never disrespected Grace__ (p. 20)

2. __Grandmother taught Grace her ABC's and numbers before age four__ (p. 22)

3. __Grandmother instilled in Grace the love of learning__ (p. 22)

Sequencing

Place a "1" on the line beside the event that happened first in Chapter Three
Place a "2" on the line beside the event that happened second in Chapter Three
and so on...

_4_ Grandmother enrolled Grace in School (p. 22-23)

_2_ Grace's mother disappeared (p. 19)

_5_ Daddy did not need Grandmother's assistance as much anymore (p. 23-24)

_1_ Grandmother adopted Grace's mother (p. 19)

_3_ Grandmother helped Daddy with Grace and her siblings (p. 19)

Identifying Cause and Effect

Entering the kindergarten class for the first time caused Grace to feel fearful. (p. 23)

What is the "Cause"? __Entering kindergarten class for the first time__

What is the "Effect"? __Grace felt fearful__

Interpreting and Evaluating Information

Place a "T" on the line beside the statements that are "true" and an "F" on the ones that are false.

__T__ Grandmother was an important influence in Grace's life (p. 24)

__F__ Grandmother often disrespected Grace (p. 20)

__T__ Grandmother instilled in Grace the love of learning (p. 22)

__T__ Grandmother made everything a learning experience (p. 22)

Name three fears Grace had about remaining in her new kindergarten class without her grandmother there? (p. 23)

1. __Would the teacher be nice to her?__
2. __Would the children like her?__
3. __Would Grandmother abandon her like her mother had done?__

Character Trait Discussion

The Character Trait for Lesson Three is "Respect"

Respect means showing kindness towards others regardless of their behavior. Having a positive attitude towards those who you like <u>and</u> those who you do not like.

Read the statement below. Then choose <u>one</u> of the questions below and answer it. Write your answer in the space provided then discuss it with your group.

Grandmother always showed "respect" towards Grace even when she misbehaved.

1. Name <u>three</u> ways Grandmother showed respect towards Grace.
2. Write about a time when someone showed "respect" towards you?
3. What are some ways we can "respect" each other.

__Answers will vary. No right or wrong answer.__

Lesson Four

This lesson coincides with Chapter Four of the book, A Gifted Child in Foster Care: A Story of Resilience
Chapter Four – "Left by Father"

Character Trait – "Dependable"

Main Idea and Supporting Details

Place an "X" on the line beside the "main idea" of the story.

_____ Grandmother did not come to help after Father left.

_____ Grace's two brothers slept in shift in front of the front door.

__X__ Daddy left Grace and her siblings in a house alone and went to Florida for work. (p. 25)

Place an "X" on the line beside the "supporting details" that are true.

__X__ Aunt Mattie brought some home-cooked food and quilts over. (p. 26)

_____ Rose came over ten times to check on the children.

__X__ It appears Daddy sent money as he had promised. (p. 26)

_____ The money stopped but the lights, gas, water, and phone remained on.

Sequencing

Place a "1" on the line beside the event that happened first in Chapter Four
Place a "2" on the line beside the event that happened second in Chapter Four
Place a "3" on the line beside the event that happened second in Chapter Four

__3__ Grace and her brothers and sisters were afraid. (p. 27)

__1__ Daddy left the children in a house alone. (p. 25)

__2__ The house the children were left in had no utilities and no phone. (p. 26)

Identifying Cause and Effect

Complete the sentence below with the correct answer.

Grace's father took her oldest brother with him when he left because…

Her oldest brother had been getting into trouble with children in the neighborhood. Daddy knew that if he left him, he could end up hurt, dead or in jail. (p. 25)

Interpreting and Evaluating Information

Review Grace's Timeline on page 93 of A Gifted Child in Foster Care: A Story of Resilience and answer the following two questions.

1. What year did Grace's father leave the children in the house alone?

   <u>   1973   </u>

2. Was it was right for him to leave? Why or why not?

   <u>   Answers will vary. No right or wrong answer.   </u>

Comparing and Contrasting

What is the difference between why Mother left and why Father left?

Why did Mother leave? (p. 15)	Why did Father leave? (p. 25)
Physical abuse / Mental illness	To look for work

Did one parent leave the children in a safer situation than the other parent? Why or why not?

<u>Yes, Mother left the children in a safer situation than Father. Mother left the children with Father. But, Father left the children in a house alone.</u>

Character Trait Discussion

The Character Trait for Lesson Four is "Dependable"

Dependable means being the type of person that others can count on. Being responsible. Keeping promises.

Answer the two questions below. Write your answers in the spaces provided then discuss them with your group.

1. Was Grace's father dependable? Why or why not?

   Answers will vary. No right or wrong answer.

   _____

   _____

   _____

   _____

   _____

   _____

   _____

   _____

   _____

2. Name three(3) ways that you can be dependable.

   1. Answers will vary. No right or wrong answer.

   2. Answers will vary. No right or wrong answer.

   3. Answers will vary. No right or wrong answer.

Lesson Five

This lesson coincides with Chapter Five of the book, A Gifted Child in Foster Care: A Story of Resilience
Chapter Five – "Living in Foster Care"

Character Trait – "Secure"

Main Idea and Supporting Details

Place an "X" on the line beside the "main idea" of the story.

    __X__ Foster care caused Grace to feel safe and secure. (p. 29)

    _____ Grandmother took care of Grace and her sister for a brief period of time.

    _____ Grace did not understand why she was chosen for the Gifted and Talented program.

Write three "supporting details" for the main idea.

1. __Grace was chosen for the Gifted and Talented program   (p. 33)__
2. __She experienced a stable home environment   (p. 32)__
3. __She learned to cook, clean up and care for herself   (p. 32)__
4. __She usually got what she wanted for Christmas   (p. 32)__
5. __She saw her father again for the first time since he left her   (p. 34)__

Sequencing

Place a "1" on the line beside the event that happened first in Chapter Five
Place a "2" on the line beside the event that happened second in Chapter Five
and so on...

    __4__ Grace lived with Big Mama. (p. 30)

    __5__ Grace was placed in her school's Gifted and Talented program. (p. 33)

    __6__ Father visited Big Mama's home. (p. 34)

    __2__ The emergency foster lady cooked a large hot breakfast for the children. (p. 29)

    __1__ The Sheriff took Grace and her brothers and sisters to an emergency foster home. (p. 29)

    __3__ Grace lived with Grandmother. (p. 30)

Identifying Cause and Effect

What caused Grandmother to leave Grace and her sister sitting on the porch until the social worker came?

They nearly destroyed her nice, clean home. They broke the seat off of the toilet stool

and ripped a window shade in the bathroom they slept in.   She could not deal with

energetic children with little home training.   (p. 30)

Interpreting and Evaluating Information

Do you feel that it was right for Grandmother to leave Grace and her sister on the porch? Why or why not?

Answers will vary. No right or wrong answer.

Comparing and Contrasting

Name one difference between the emergency foster home and the home Grace was left in.

The emergency foster home provided food for Grace, but the home she was left in had no

food. Grace felt safe at the emergency foster home, but she felt afraid in the home she was

left in. Other answers are possible.

Character Trait Discussion

The Character Trait for Lesson Five is "Secure".

Secure means feeling safe; not feeling fearful.

Read the five questions below. Then answer one of the questions. Write your answer in the space provided then discuss it with your group.

1. Did Grace feel "secure" in the home her father left her in? Why or why not? (p. 27)
2. Did Grace feel "secure" at the emergency foster home? Why or why not? (p. 29)

3. Did Grace feel "secure" living with Grandmother? Why or why not? (p. 30)
4. Did Grace feel "secure" living with Big Mama? Why or why not? (p. 32)
5. Did Grace feel "secure" in the Gifted and Talented classroom? Why or why not? (p. 33)

Answers will vary. No right or wrong answer.

Bonus Discussion

Read the statement and answer the question below. Write your answer in the space provided then discuss it with your group.

Grace did not talk about how she felt about seeing her father after eighteen months. What feeling(s) do you think she felt? Why?

    Answers will vary. No right or wrong answer.

_____

_____

_____

_____

_____

_____

_____

_____

_____

_____

_____

_____

_____

_____

Lesson Six

This lesson coincides with Chapter Six of the book, A Gifted Child in Foster Care: A Story of Resilience
Chapter Six – "Separated From Siblings"

Character Trait – "Love"

Main Idea and Supporting Details

Place an "X" on the line beside the "main idea" of the story.

_____ Birth order played a big part in the way each child was affected by being separated.

_____ Terrance served in the United States Army.

__X__ Grace was separated from all but one of her siblings during foster care. (p. 37)

Write three "supporting details" for the main idea.

1. Grace visited her siblings three times during her three years in foster care   (p. 37)

2. Danisha lived with Big Mama at the same time as Grace did   (p. 37)

3. Each of Grace's siblings influenced her   (p. 41)

Sequencing

Name Grace's siblings from youngest to oldest.

1. Danisha   (p. 37)

2. Terrance   (p. 37)

3. Carla   (p. 38)

4. Grayson   (p. 38)

5. Jerome   (p. 39)

Identifying Cause and Effect

Read the following statement and answer the question below.

In Chapter Six Grace stated, "Excitement gripped me when I knew I was going to visit my siblings." (p. 37)

What caused Grace to feel excitement? <u>Knowing she was going to visit her siblings.</u>

Interpreting and Evaluating Information

Review Grace's Timeline on page 93 of A Gifted Child in Foster Care: A Story of Resilience and answer the following question:

What year did Grace begin living with Big Mama? <u>1973</u>

<u>Name the sibling who also lived with Big Mama.</u> Danisha (p. 37)

Write <u>three</u> things that Grace remembers about that sibling. (p. 37)

1. <u>She was quiet.</u>
2. <u>She made good grades.</u>
3. <u>She always got the jobs she applied for.</u>
4. <u>She was neat and clean.</u>

<u>Name the sibling who had the greatest influence on Grace.</u> Jerome (p. 37)

Why was that sibling's influence so great? <u>He was protective and taught Grace how to fistfight. He was determined to keep his siblings from being hurt by the cruel world. (p. 40)</u>

Comparing and Contrasting

Choose two of Grace's siblings and write their names on the lines in the circles below.
Now, name two ways the siblings named above are different and one way they are the same.

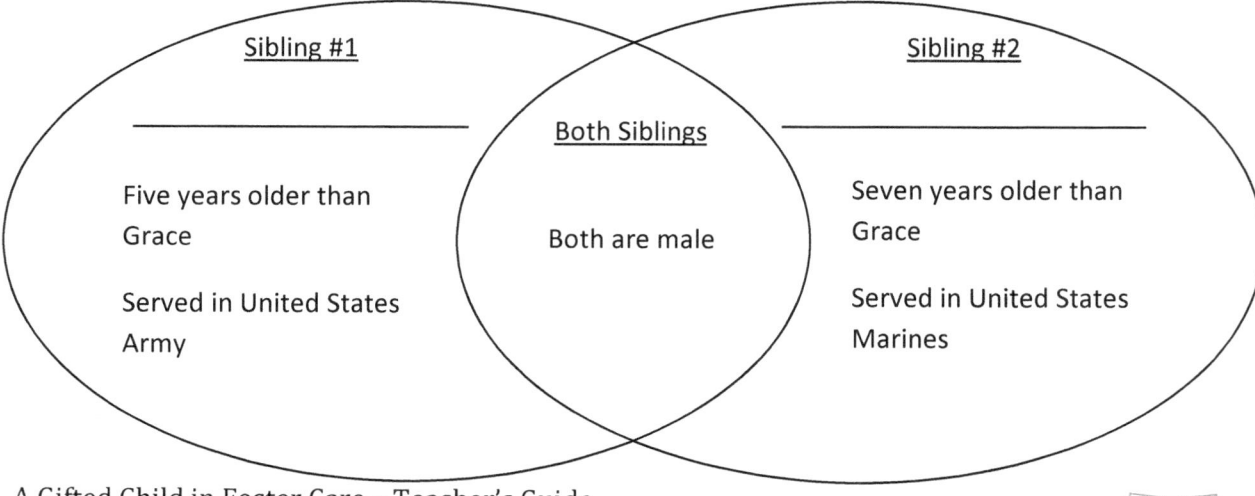

Sibling #1: Five years older than Grace; Served in United States Army

Both Siblings: Both are male

Sibling #2: Seven years older than Grace; Served in United States Marines

A Gifted Child in Foster Care – Teacher's Guide
© Inspirations by Grace LaJoy, LLC

Character Trait Discussion

The Character Trait for Lesson Six is "Love"

Love means caring about someone, having kind thoughts about them, and appreciating the positive affect they have had on your life.

Answer the two questions below. Write your answers in the space provided then discuss them with your group.

Do you feel Grace loved her sisters and brothers? Why or why not?

____Answers will vary. No right or wrong answer._____

_____

_____

_____

_____

_____

_____

_____

_____

Name three things you can do to show someone you love them.

1. ____Answers will vary. No right or wrong answer._____

2. _____

3. _____

Lesson Seven

This lesson coincides with Chapter Seven of the book, A Gifted Child in Foster Care: A Story of Resilience
Chapter Seven – "A Typical Day in Foster Care"

Character Trait – "Obedience"

Main Idea and Supporting Details

Place an "X" on the line beside the "main idea" of the story.

_____ Grace liked visiting the school library.

__X__ Grace had a daily routine, which included various chores while living in foster care. (p. 43)

_____ If Big Mama was not happy, nobody was happy.

Write three "supporting details" for the main idea.

1. __Grace performed daily chores such as making her bed and cleaning the bathroom.__ (p. 43)

2. __Mornings at Big Mama's house were challenging.   (p. 44)__

3. __The first thing Grace did after school was started on her homework.   (p. 47)__

Sequencing

A typical day in foster care included the nine activities below. What order did Grace do each activity listed below?

Place a "1" on the line next to the activity that Grace did first.
Place a "2" on the line next to the activity that Grace did second.
and so on…

__8__ Took a bath (p. 47)   __7__ Played outside (p. 47)

__1__ Ate breakfast (p. 45)   __2__ Walked to school (p. 45)

__9__ Went to bed (p. 47)   __6__ Completed chores (p. 48)

__3__ Walked home from school (p. 46)   __4__ Started on homework (p. 47)

__5__ Ate dinner (p. 47)

Identifying Cause and Effect

Read the two questions below, then write the correct answer in the space provided.

1. What was the "effect" when Tina and Grace did not clean up correctly?
   <u> Big Mama corrected them   (p. 43)   </u>

2. What caused Big Mama to have a bad mood?

   <u> When the girls made too much noise and woke her up in the mornings   (p. 44) </u>

   _____

Interpreting and Evaluating Information

Write <u>three</u> things that Grace liked most about school. (p. 45)

1. <u> Going to the school library   </u>

2. <u> Playing kickball at recess   </u>

3. <u> Going on field trips   </u>

Name <u>one</u> reason why Grace chose books that were easy to read when she went to the school library.

<u> Chapter books took too long to get to the ending.   (p. 45)   </u>

<u> She liked to know as soon as possible how the story worked out.   (p. 45) </u>

<u> She did not care for all the detail and drama in longer books.   (p. 45-46) </u>

<u> She did not feel she read as fast as other students.   (p. 46)   </u>

Comparing and Contrasting

Fill in the blanks below with the correct words.

Whereas Danisha was Grace's <u> real </u> sister, Tina was Grace's <u> foster </u> sister. (p. 46)

Character Trait Discussion

The Character Trait for Lesson Seven is "Obedience"

Obedience means doing what your parent, teacher, or other authority figure instructs you to do. Doing the right thing.

Read the two instructions below. Write your answers to both in the space provided then discuss them with your group.

Name three ways Grace was obedient.

1. ___Answers will vary. No right or wrong answer._____
2. ___Answers will vary. No right or wrong answer._____
3. ___Answers will vary. No right or wrong answer._____

Name three ways you can be obedient.

1. ___Answers will vary. No right or wrong answer._____
2. ___Answers will vary. No right or wrong answer._____
3. ___Answers will vary. No right or wrong answer._____

Bonus Discussion

What are your thoughts about Big Mama telling Grace she could not eat breakfast anymore? Write your thoughts in the space below then discuss it with your group.

___Answers will vary. No right or wrong answer._____

_____

_____

_____

_____

Lesson Eight

This lesson coincides with Chapter Eight of the book, A Gifted Child in Foster Care: A Story of Resilience
Chapter Eight – "How Foster Care Shaped My Life"

Character Trait – "Content"

Main Idea and Supporting Details

Place an "X" on the line beside the "main idea" of the story.

　　__X__　Foster care met Grace's social, physical, mental and emotional needs. (p. 49)

　　_____　Big Mama took Grace to the drive-in.

　　_____　Grace has stability in her life today.

Write three "supporting details" for the main idea.

1. __Foster care gave Grace a stable place to live   (p. 51)__

2. __Grace received health and dental care while in foster care   (p. 51)__

3. __Grace learned the proper way to do chores while in foster care   (p. 50)__

Identifying Cause and Effect

Place an "X" on the line beside the correct answer.

　　What caused Grace to finally appreciate all the good things Big Mama did for her?

　　__X__　She began to see how her time spent in foster care contributed to the stability she enjoys in her life today. (p. 51)

　　_____　She realized her children were thankful for Big Mama.

Interpreting and Evaluating Information

Unscramble the answers to the following question.

　　What *five* things did foster care offer Grace? (p. 51)

1. bsleat mheo rnotnenemiv

　　__stable__　　　　　　__home__　　　　　　__environment__

A Gifted Child in Foster Care – Teacher's Guide
© Inspirations by Grace LaJoy, LLC

2. lfmyia   iiistcavet

   __family__   __activities__

3. natoientt

   __attention__

4. thhlae & tdlaen rcae

   __health__ & __dental__ __care__

5. plseidnici

   __discipline__

Comparing and Contrasting

Name <u>three</u> differences between Grace's life during foster care and after foster care.

During Foster Care	After Foster Care
Grace went fishing and to picnics (p. 49)	Grace had no outside family activities
Grace had a stable home environment (p. 51)	Grace had an unstable home environment
Grace had stable friendships (p. 50)	Grace found it difficult to develop friendships

Character Trait Discussion

The Character Trait for Lesson Eight is "Content"

Content means being happy with what you have and not worrying about what you don't have. Appreciating the good things in your life.

Answer <u>one</u> of the questions below. Write your answer in the space provided then discuss it with your group.

1. Was Grace "content" during foster care? Why or why not?
2. Are you "content"? Why or why not?
3. Name three things you could say to encourage someone who is not "content" with their life.

   Answers will vary. No right or wrong answer.

Lesson Nine

This lesson coincides with Chapter Nine of the book, A Gifted Child in Foster Care: A Story of Resilience
Chapter Nine – "Life After Foster Care"

Character Trait – "Courage"

Main Idea and Supporting Details

Place an "X" on the line beside the "main idea" of the story.

_____ Grace got in more fights after foster care.

_____ Grace went to school with gangsters and children who carried weapons.

__X__ Grace's father finally met the requirements to take her out of foster care. (p. 53)

Write three "supporting details" for the main idea.

1. __Grace began sixth grade in North Carolina__ (p. 54)

2. __Grace went to school with gangsters__ (p. 55)

3. __Grace got into fights__ (p. 56)

Sequencing

Place a "1" on the line next to the event that happened first.
Place a "2" on the line next to the event that happened second.
and so on...

__3__ Grace met her father's girlfriend, Ms. Ruby. (p. 53)

__4__ Grace's father took her to the three bedroom townhome where they would be living. (p. 54)

__5__ Grace began sixth grade in North Carolina. (p. 54)

__2__ Grace and her sisters rode the bus from Kansas City, Missouri to Charlotte, North Carolina. (p. 53)

__6__ Grace's father moved them back and forth several times. (p. 55)

__1__ Father met state requirements to get Grace out of foster care. (p. 53)

Identifying Cause and Effect

Place an "X" on the line beside the correct answer.

What caused Tracy to want to fight Grace?
_____ She wanted Grace to be a part of her gang.
__X__ She believed Grace was taking all of her boyfriends. (p. 55)

Interpreting and Evaluating Information

Read the following question and write your answer on the line below.

What feeling do you think Grace felt while going to school with gangsters?

_____Fear_____

Comparing and Contrasting

Read the following question and write your answer on the line below.

Why does Grace believe she got into fights *after* going to live with her father, but did not have fights *while* in foster care? (p. 57)

____Because in foster care, she lived in a stable home environment for three years which gave

her time to develop secure friendships with classmates. With her father, she moved

around a lot which made it difficult to develop any friendships before moving again.____

Character Trait Discussion

The Character Trait for Lesson Nine is "Courage"

Courage means not being afraid. Being confident.

Answer one of the three questions below. Write your answer in the space provided then discuss it with your group.

1. Do you feel Grace had courage? Why or why not?
2. Describe a situation in which you displayed courage.
3. Describe a situation in which someone you know displayed courage.

Answers will vary. No right or wrong answer.

Lesson Ten

This lesson coincides with Chapter Ten of the book, A Gifted Child in Foster Care: A Story of Resilience
Chapter Ten – "Daddy Left Again"

Character Trait – "Encouragement"

Main Idea and Supporting Details

Place an "X" on the line beside the "main idea" of the story.

____X____ After Daddy got Grace out of foster care, he left again. (p. 59)

_____ Grace's life was threatened when she was thirteen years old.

_____ Daddy had good intentions and would never say anything to hurt Grace.

Write three "supporting details" for the main idea.

1. ____When Daddy left again, he left Grace with a lady in North Carolina____ (p. 59)

2. ____Grace's English teacher noticed her writing ability____ (p. 62)

3. ____Grace's life was threatened when she was thirteen year old____ (p. 59)

Sequencing

Place a "1" on the line next to the event that happened first.
Place a "2" on the line next to the event that happened second.
and so on…

____3____ Grace's teacher noticed her writing ability. (p. 62)

____1____ Daddy left again. (p. 59)

____4____ Grace realized she was not "hard-headed". (p. 64)

____2____ Grace lived with Carla in a townhome. (p. 59)

Identifying Cause and Effect

Read the following question and write your answer in the space below.

What does Grace believe caused her grades to drop and to never again be recognized as a "gifted" student?

<u>After foster care, she no longer had anyone who encouraged her to do her homework.</u>

_____

_____

_____

_____

_____

_____

Interpreting and Evaluating Information

Review Grace's Timeline on page 93 of A Gifted Child in Foster Care: A Story of Resilience and answer the following question.

What year did Daddy leave Grace in North Carolina? <u> 1979 </u>

Comparing and Contrasting

Why did Daddy leave again?

<u> To travel to look for cement work.   (p. 59) </u>

_____

Was Daddy's reason for leaving the second time the *same* or *different* from his reason for leaving the first time? (See Chapter Four for the reason Daddy left the first time) (p. 25)

<u> Same </u>

Character Trait Discussion

The Character Trait for Lesson Ten is "Encouragement"

Encouragement means saying or doing something to cause someone to believe they can be successful.

Answer one of the questions below. Write your answer in the space provided then discuss it with your group.

1. What did Grace's English teacher do to "encourage" her?
2. What did the high school principal say that made Grace feel encouraged?
3. Write three things you can say to encourage a friend or a classmate?

#1 – The English teacher noticed Grace's creative writing ability and complimented her in front of the entire class. (p. 62)

#2 – The principal said, "No, you are not hard-headed." (p. 64)

#3 – Answers will vary. No right or wrong answer.

Lesson Eleven

This lesson coincides with Chapter Eleven of the book, A Gifted Child in Foster Care: A Story of Resilience
Chapter Eleven – "Pregnant at Seventeen"

Character Trait – "Diligence"

Main Idea and Supporting Details

Place an "X" on the line beside the "main idea" of the story.

_____ Grace used her creative writing talent.

_____ Kansas City is a great place for a teenage girl to live.

__X__ Grace became a young mother of a baby girl. (p. 69)

Write three "supporting details" for the main idea.

1. Grace began attending a local community college in the fall of 1984. (p. 69)

2. Grace did not have a clue how tough being a single parent would be. (p. 69)

3. Grace learned she could still be successful in life. (p. 73)

Sequencing

Place a "1" on the line next to the event that Grace did first.
Place a "2" on the line next to the event that Grace did second.
and so on…

__5__ Began attending a local community college (p. 69)

__2__ Won homecoming queen (p. 67)

__4__ Became pregnant (p. 68)

__6__ Gave birth to Arica (p. 69)

__3__ Used her creative writing skills (p. 67)

__1__ Began her senior year in Kansas City (p. 67)

Identifying Cause and Effect

Read the following question and write your answer in the space below.

What *caused* Grace to leave her first apartment with her baby?

_____She discovered it was infested with mice.   (p. 70)_____

_____

_____

_____

Interpreting and Evaluating Information

Grace became a mother at age eighteen.

Using the glossary on pages 97-99 of A Gifted Child in Foster Care: A Story of Resilience, write the definition for the word "mother" in the space below.

_____Mother – A female who gives birth to a child.   (p. 98)_____

_____

_____

Comparing and Contrasting
Fill in the blanks below with the correct words.

Whereas Grace attended school in ____North____ ____Carolina____ in the eleventh grade, she attended school in ____Kansas____ ____City____ during her last year of high school. (p. 67)

Character Trait Discussion
The Character Trait for Lesson Eleven is "Diligence"

Diligence means to keep trying to be successful even when things are hard. Overcoming an obstacle or a challenge.

Answer <u>one</u> of the four questions below. Write your answer in the space provided then discuss it with your group.

1. In what way was Grace diligent?
2. How did Grace's diligence affect her children?
3. Name an obstacle or challenge that you have overcome? What did you do to overcome it?
4. Name a person you know who has been diligent. What did that person do to overcome their obstacle or challenge?

___Answers will vary. No right or wrong answer._____

Lesson Twelve

This lesson coincides with Chapter Twelve of the book, A Gifted Child in Foster Care: A Story of Resilience **Chapter Twelve – "My Gift Revealed"**

Character Trait – "Insight"

Main Idea and Supporting Details

Place an "X" on the line beside the "main idea" of the story.

_____ Grace was abandoned by her mother and her father

___X___ Grace's realized writing was her gift and began to use it. (p. 76)

_____ Grace volunteered as Youth Department Director.

Write three "supporting details" for the main idea.

1. ___Grace discovered she had written over two hundred poems and thirty-five songs.___ (p. 75)

2. ___An unemployment specialist saw something special about Grace.___ (p. 75)

3. ___People began to be empowered by Grace's writing. She received numerous compliments.___ (p. 76)

Sequencing

Place a "1" on the line next to the event that happened first in Chapter Twelve.
Place a "2" on the line next to the event that happened second in Chapter Twelve.
and so on...

___3___ Grace published her fist book of poetry (p. 76)

___1___ Grace often wondered what her gift was (p. 75)

___4___ Grace helped other writers to become authors (p. 77)

___2___ Grace volunteered as Youth Drama Director (p. 76)

Identifying Cause and Effect

Read the following question. Write your answer in the space below.

What caused Grace to be shaped into the person she is today?

    <u>Events such as being abandoned by her mother and father and living in foster care.</u>

    <u>(p. 27)</u>

Interpreting and Evaluating Information
Fill in the blanks with the correct words.

The <u>punishments</u> while in foster care instilled the discipline Grace needs today to create her <u>vision</u>, accomplish her <u>goals</u>, and fulfill her <u>purpose</u>. (p. 78)

Comparing and Contrasting
Answer the following question in the space provided below.

How is Grace's life different now than it would have been if her story had been different.

<u>She would have never had the opportunity to experience being "a gifted child in foster</u>

<u>care." (p. 78)</u>

Character Trait Discussion
The Character Trait for Lesson Twelve is "Insight"

Insight means seeing something good in the midst of a bad situation. Seeing something positive about a person that the person does not see yet.

Answer <u>one</u> of the questions below. Write your answer in the space provided then discuss it with your group.

1. What insight did Grace gain from other people about her gift?
2. What insight did Grace gain as a result of being chosen for the gifted and talented program?
3. Describe a time when you, or someone you know, saw something good in the midst of a bad situation.

Answers will vary. No right or wrong answer.

Lesson Thirteen

This lesson coincides with Chapter Thirteen of the book, A Gifted Child in Foster Care: A Story of Resilience Chapter Thirteen – "Empowerment for Children"

Character Trait – "Forgiveness"

Interpreting and Evaluating Information

Read the two questions below and place and "X" on the line next to the correct answer.

1. What did Grace have to let go of in order to walk into her successful future?

    _____ Her best friend
    __X__ Her painful past (p. 79)
    _____ Her dog

2. How long did Grace dwell on the negative, hurtful things after she left foster care?

    _____ Five months
    __X__ Thirty years (p. 79)
    _____ Ten years

Circle all of the correct responses.

What positive things did Grace dwell on that caused her to truly let go of the negative experiences? (p. 80)

Stable home environment	**Being "smart" or "gifted"**
Her beauty	Having a brand new bike
Good physical hygiene	Being an unwed mother
Going to church	**Learning to cook**
Proper housekeeping	**Regular health care**

Fill in the blanks below with the correct words.

1. The best way to start moving _____forward_____ is to _____refrain_____ from looking back. (p. 80)

2. If used effectively, your life experiences will make you _____stronger_____ and _____empower_____ others. (p. 80)

True or False
Write a "T" on the line next to the statement below if it is true and an "F" if it is false.

__T__ Three things you can do to use your life experiences effectively are: Recognize your power, be confident, and take advantage of opportunities. (p. 80)

__T__ You were born for a purpose and you should never give up. (p. 81)

Character Trait Discussion
The Character Trait for Lesson Thirteen is "Forgiveness"

Forgiveness to let go of negative past experiences and move forward. To release someone of something they did to hurt you. To show love toward someone who has done something wrong.

Chose one of the three questions below. Write your answer in the space provided then discuss it with your group.

1. What caused forgiveness to be released in Grace's heart? Who did she have to forgive?

2. Think of someone who hurt you. Have you forgiven that person? If so, how were you able to do it? If not, why not?

3. Do you feel forgiveness is important? Why or why not?

   Answers will vary. No right or wrong answer.

Lesson Fourteen

This lesson coincides with Chapter Fourteen of the book, A Gifted Child in Foster Care: A Story of Resilience Chapter Fourteen – "Empowerment for Parents"

Character Trait – "Building Self-esteem"

Interpreting and Evaluating Information

Read the question below and place and "X" on the line next to the correct answer.

1. What is a "gift"?

   _____ A birthday present

   _____ Doing something nice for someone

   __X__ An unlearned talent (p. 83)

*Circle **all** of the correct responses.*

Which of the following steps will help parents empower their child?

   Buying their child a pet

   Paying attention to what their child enjoys (p. 83)

   Recognizing what their child is naturally good at (p. 83)

   Giving their child money

   Knowing that they have the power to shape their child's life (p. 85)

Fill in the blanks below with the correct words.

1. All children are _____gifted_____ in one way or another. (p. 83)
2. One who has a gift _____enjoys_____ using it. (p. 83)

True or False
Write a "T" on the line next to the statement below if it is true and an "F" if it is false.

   __T__ Parents should provide opportunities for their child to participate in the thing he/she enjoys. (p. 84)

   __F__ You should not pursue your gift unless it will cause you to make a lot of money. (p. 85)

Character Trait Discussion
The Character Trait for Lesson Fourteen is "Building Self-esteem"

Building Self-esteem means doing or saying something to empower someone to know that they are important. Assuring someone that they have the power to do great things.

Chose one of the three questions below. Write your answer in the space provided then discuss it with your group.

1. Parents can build their children's self esteem by helping them to recognize that they have a gift. Can you think of other ways parents can help build children's self-esteem?

2. What are two things your teacher can say or do to help build your self-esteem?

3. What are three things you can do or say to help build someone else's self-esteem?

   Answers will vary. No right or wrong answer.

Bonus Character Trait Discussion

The Bonus Character Trait is "Determination"

Determination means refusing to give up regardless of obstacles. Doing everything in your power to complete a task.

Choose one of the three questions below and answer it. Write your answer in the space provided then discuss it with your group.

1. Have you ever had determination to achieve a goal?
   If yes, write that goal below and explain how you achieved it.
2. What future goals have you made for yourself? How do you plan to achieve them?
3. Do you feel "determination" is important? Why or why not?

    Answers will vary. No right or wrong answer.

Advanced Reading Comprehension Skills

After reading the story, students may practice these *advanced* reading comprehension skills:

1. Describe each main character in the student's own words.

2. Make predictions about the future of the main characters.

3. Discuss how they feel the author displayed "resilience".

4. Make assumptions about why they feel the author wrote the book.

5. Analyze the author's purpose for writing A Gifted Child in Foster Care.

6. Read, analyze and discuss the poem entitled, "He's Worth It" on pages 86 and 87.

7. Compare and contrast A Gifted Child in Foster Care with another book.

Additional Lesson Ideals

A Gifted Child in Foster Care: *A Story of Resilience* can enhance academic achievement and assist with Project Based Learning within the classroom.

It can be used in conjunction with the four core curriculum areas:

- Language Arts
- Mathematics
- Science/Technology
- Social Studies

It can also be used in conjunction with:

- Career Preparatory
- Journalism/Communication Arts

Students will practice the following skills:

Reading   Writing   Comprehension   Problem Solving   Critical Thinking   Analytical

These skills will be enhanced when students perform each of the lesson ideas below.
Note: These projects can be completed individually or in small or large group settings.

Language Arts

Lesson Ideas:

- Create a "table of contents" from their own memoir.
- Write their own memoir.
- Write a book report or book review.
- Discuss individual chapters from the book in small group settings.
- Select five or more words and define them using the glossary in the back of the book
- Choose three topics to research using the index in the back of the book
- Have a group discussion, or write a report about, the following:
    - What gift did the author Have? How did she use her gift to help others?
    - What gift do you have? How can you use your gift to help others?

Mathematics

Lesson Ideas:

- Create a timeline of their life (using author's timeline in back of book as an example)
- Create word problems using dates and events from the author's life (i.e. If author was born in 1966, what was her age when she when she entered into foster care in 1973?)

Science

Lesson Ideas:

- Use internet search engines to learn ways to conserve energy by "going green".
- Name three things their family can do to keep utilities (gas, water, lights) from being shut off.
- Comparing and Contrasting the weather between North Carolina, Missouri, and Michigan.
(the states where the author lived)

Technology

Lesson Ideas:

- Use the internet to research information about foster care.
- Use the computer word processor to type reports pertaining to the author's story.

Social Studies

Lesson Ideas:

- Discuss, in a small or large group setting, how the author's life has positively affected the world
- Think about something they can do to positively affect their school, home, or community.
- Work in small groups to create a timeline of a historical person.
    (use author's timeline as an example)
- Point out, on a globe or map of the world, all the states the author lived
- Draw a map of each state in which the author lived

Career Preparatory

Lesson Ideas:

➢ Research careers in writing; report on the skills and training required; report on the salary
➢ Discuss, in a group setting, when and how the author first began to turn her writing gift into a career

Journalism/Communication Arts

Lesson Ideas:

➢ Write a press release or news story about the author and the book
➢ Design three interview questions you would want to ask the author
➢ Write a speech about the life and work of the author

A Gifted Child in Foster Care: *A Story of Resilience*
BOOK – ISBN: 978-1-7341868-0-2
REVISED EDITION

A great reading source for teachers, counselors and students. It is a true story of hope, determination, and overcoming adversity.

In this book, Dr. Grace LaJoy shares her life story of being deserted by her mother, living in foster care, and ending up in a gifted and talented class while still in foster care.

A Gifted Child in Foster Care: *A Story of Resilience*
STUDENT WORKBOOK – ISBN: 978-1-7341868-1-9
REVISED EDITION

The lessons in this workbook will improve reading comprehension for students, while changing attitudes and building character.

Students will read the chapters in the nonfiction book, A Gifted Child in Foster Care: A Story of Resilience, individually or as a group. Then they will do the lessons from this workbook that coincides with each chapter.

A Gifted Child in Foster Care: *A Story of Resilience*
TEACHER'S GUIDE – ISBN: 978-1-7341868-2-6
REVISED EDITION

This workbook for students will assist teachers in fulfilling the state requirements of the Grade-Level Expectations for Communication/Language Arts.

Teachers will be able to lead students in critical thinking exercises. Students will be able to develop and apply skills and strategies to comprehend, analyze and evaluate nonfiction.

The Teacher's Guide contains the answers to the lesson activities in the Student Workbook.

When Grace LaJoy originally published her foster care story, *A Gifted Child in Foster Care*, she thought she would *never* find her mother. But, she found her after 49 years! Now she is sharing her fascinating journey in an inspiring series you will love!

Titles include:
Finding Mother after Five Decades: *A Story of Hope*
Reuniting with Mother: *A Story of Tenacity*
After the Reunion: *A Story of Acceptance*
Diary of Emotions: *Thoughts and Feelings*

Discussion Questions in the back of each book are designed to increase awareness and discussion about mental health.

Questions Teachers Can Ask aid in increasing reading comprehension skills in the classroom.

This inspiring series offers hope to anyone searching for a lost loved one. You enjoyed Grace LaJoy's foster care story. Now, collect the entire Finding Mother Series today!

Available in softcover and Kindle eBook
Collect them all at Amazon.com
www.gracelajoy.com

Finding Mother after Five Decades: A Story of Hope
Grace LaJoy's determination pays off when she finally finds her mother who abandoned her at age two. Discover the specific details of her intriguing journey in *Finding Mother after Five Decades*, BOOK 1 of the Finding Mother Series

Reuniting with Mother: A Story of Tenacity
What happens when Grace LaJoy and her siblings come face-to-face with their estranged mother after 49 years? How does she receive them? Find out in *Reuniting with Mother*, BOOK 2 of the Finding Mother Series

After the Reunion: A Story of Acceptance
After a very emotional reunion, Grace LaJoy has two concerns to address with her long-lost mother. What are her concerns? Does she get the answers she needs from her mother? Find out in *After the Reunion*, BOOK 3 of the Finding Mother Series

Diary of Emotion: Thoughts and Feelings
After reuniting with her mother after 49 years, Grace LaJoy toils with an array of thoughts and feeling. She reveals them all in *Diary of Emotions*, BOOK 4 of the Finding Mother Series

www.ingramcontent.com/pod-product-compliance
Lightning Source LLC
Chambersburg PA
CBHW051423070526
44584CB00023B/3548